SERENDIPITY

by

Michael James Cook

SERENDIPITY: 978-1-5272-4388-0

Writer and Author is Mr Michael James Cook
Designed and Published by Virtual Admin UK -
www.virtualadminuk.co.uk
Printed by Ex Why Zed - www.exwhyzed.co.uk

SERENDIPITY

To dear Hazel,
With much love
and happy memories
from Mike .
xx

DEDICATED TO:

Emily, Sophie, Lucy, Libby and Olivia,
with much love.

ABOUT THE AUTHOR

Michael James Cook was born in North Reddish, Stockport, Cheshire and was educated at Stockport School and the universities of Durham, Bristol and Exeter. A promising career in professional sport was dashed at an early age by a serious knee injury. He was an ordinand of the Church of England and a full-time Youth Leader in Bristol. He was the first full-time Teacher/Youth and Community Leader to be appointed in Cheshire. He also taught Religious and Social Education in secondary modern, comprehensive and grammar schools in Devon, Durham, Essex and Somerset for almost thirty years. When he took early retirement from teaching, he and his wife owned and ran the village shop at Kirkby Mallory in Leicestershire for ten years. He took the F.A. Coaching course when he was a young man and was for many years a part-time soccer scout for a number of Football League clubs; soccer remaining the first love of his life. His many interests, apart from writing poetry, include sport, theology, geology, philately and preserved steam railways. He is a published author, photographer and songwriter.

"Teachers
know not when their pupils see the light".

Michael J. Cook (1987)

CONTENTS

Preface

Acknowledgement
Appendix
Published Elsewhere

PREFACE

Just as an old footballer becomes increasingly aware it is time for him to hang up his boots, so I, after sixty years of writing poems, since the age of seventeen, have come to realise it is time for me to hang up my pen(s). This really is my final anthology. All my poems will have been published and my mission accomplished. It has been a long journey since Mile End.

At primary school, I was hopeless at English and my teacher in the Scholarship Class was Miss Pass who considered me to be her Master Failure. Even at grammar school I always felt inferior to the other pupils where English was concerned. I passed GCE 'O' level French but failed English Language and had to resit it in the November. Fortunately, I passed and my journey began. I had a religious experience while out hiking with friends in the Peak District and started writing a book about religion for teenagers, which was later published by a London publisher two years later when I was nineteen years of age. Almost simultaneously I met a girl while on holiday with friends at Scarborough. She inspired me to write a few poems for the first time in my life. The rest, as they say, is history.

While I was a student at Bede College, Durham University I discovered I was very good at writing essays, so much so that I wrote some for other students and charged them half a crown a time (12 ½ pence in today's money). This enabled me to see my girlfriend in Newcastle twice instead of once a week. The money was well spent because the same Geordie lass I met in Scarborough later became my wife. This year we will be celebrating 57 years of married life.

In my final year at Bede College, I wrote a 52,000 word dissertation entitled "Towards A Christian Education", which the college encouraged me to try and get published. It was accepted by London Publishers, Darton, Longman and Todd, only for it to be shelved at the last minute because a rival publisher published a book at the same time on the same subject written by a leading academic in the field.

Once I started teaching, I wrote Lesson Notes for the Scripture Union to supplement my income. I also completed the British and American School of Writing course on Short Story Writing. About this time, I started writing the first of the 56 songs I have written and more poems, both of which I used as teaching aids in school.

Later, while teaching at Axminster a man named Howard Sergeant, who was later awarded the MBE for services to Literature, offered to subsidise my first anthology of poems in 1975. He did the same for my second one in 1976 and the third one in 1977. Unfortunately, I wasn't adopted by a mainstream publisher as some of his previous prodigies had been. I switched to photography and abandoned poetry.

However, a few years later I was approached by Thomas Nelson and Sons Ltd, a mainstream publisher who wanted to produce a book of my poems and songs for schools. Once again, this came to nothing due to the publisher experiencing difficulties during the recession at the time.

In the past few years, declining health has made me endeavour to get as many of my poems published as possible. It is said that there are over 2 million people in Britain writing poetry. I don't know how true that is but I do know it is the least lucrative genre of all. I found it very therapeutic at times and useful as a teaching aid. It has its highs and lows but most people write poetry simply because they find they can and they enjoy it. Once that comes to an end it is time to stop. My poetry is a gift I received. My only wish is that others should enjoy it too.

M.J.C
Hinckley 2019

ON THE SHELF

If you should see me on a shelf
Looking lost, all by myself,
Please pick me up and take a look,
I'm not like any other book.

Inside you'll find the reason why
I can make you laugh or cry;
Be your friend for many a day,
Either at work or when you play.

I'm full of verses penned with care,
Poetic thoughts I'll gladly share,
So don't pass by without a glance,
Some loves are born as if by chance.

2018

ASPIRING POET

Michael James Cook
Set out to write a poetry book.
As words flowed from verse to verse
His poems grew steadily worse.

Note: The poem is an example of a Clerihew which is a
       four lined poem rhyming aabb. It is supposed to
       begin with the name of the person to be discussed
       or described. It was invented by Edmund Clerihew
       Bentley. The lines must be of unequal syllabic
       length and the result is intended to be risible.

1982

SPINSTER'S SOLILOQUY

A miss by name complete
And missed always by life.
A maiden aunt, a friend, a guest -
Not once a bride or wife.

Evenings I spend alone.
Put out the cat and pause,
Sit down, go round the flat again;
Slippers on feet like claws.

I read armchair romance
About sweet love and flowers.
A virgin's mouth with cups of tea
Sipping away the hours.

I neither smoke nor drink.
I hope I have no sin.
I take no chance at all to lose
And so can't hope to win.

1978

COME TOGETHER

Meeting you
Wanting you
Lustful sighs.
Chance a miss,
Steal a kiss
Catch your eye.
Sex invites
Age divides,
Love provides.
Snap greetings
Hopes leaping,
Sad "goodbyes".
Bright flowers
Lonely hours
Passing by.
Hidden notions
Blocked emotions,
Wondering why.
Words deceiving
Off-hand dealings,
Compounded lies.
Actions adding
Guilt subtracting,
Passion multiplied.
Emotional pain
Conflicting aims,
Needs compromised.
Purple patches
Golden fractures
In a winter's sky.

Days of pleasure,
Gifts to treasure,
Money can't buy.
Poetic Rhymes
Romantic times
Which fate supplies.
Flesh embracing,
Faith performing
Miracles inside.
Senses blooding,
Urges flooding,
Ecstatic sighs.
The devil's dam
Tempted Adam
Innocence died.
The laws of men
The censor's pen
Stems not the tide.
In vacant space
There is a place
Where lust abides.
Mother Nature
Orders reason
To stand aside.
So come, let's fly
Across an unknown sky
To a life we cannot deny.

1975

SLEEPY HEAD

Rest awhile, think awhile, sleepy head.
Take your time, know you're mine, till I'm dead.
When you go, I feel low, like I said,
So rest awhile, sleepy head, in my arms.

Hold my hand, squeeze my hand, little one.
Please don't say that I may have no fun.
Play your part and your heart will be won,
So hold my hand, little one, while we talk.

Close your eyes, hush your sighs, sleepy head.
Don't you know it's time to go, time for bed?
Who can see for you and me what lies ahead?
So close your eyes, sleepy head, in my arms.

1964

A DAY IN THE LIFE

A third of life is lost in sleep,
A third is spent in play.
The fraction left is used up working
The common denominator
Day.

1971

BLOW IT

No fun to be abed
To doze and fry
With raging head.

No fun to wake and sigh
As those at home
Leave you to die.

No fun to ache alone
At war with germs
Inside your bones

No fun when eyelids burn
And others gloat
It's now your turn.

No fun a red raw throat
Hot steaming nose
Slit eyes afloat.

Like ice on white-hot coals,
No fun a flu-like cold.

1977

OMENS OF DEATH

The approach of the Grim Reaper
May be heralded by a dog howling
Outside a house at night,
Or a live adder on a doorstep;
A crow flying thrice overhead;
A white pigeon on the roof;
A raven screeching or an owl hooting.
And in the garden you may see
A flower blooming out of season,
Or one remaining apple on the tree.
A cock may crow at the midnight hour,
A church bell toll which hasn't been rung.
And should a candle be burning blue
Or a black beetle run over your shoe,
A picture fall from its nail untouched
Or scissors point to earth when dropped,
Then will the omens of death be in view.
And should you witness a falling star,
Or the fearsome doppelgänger appear
Like the phantom Drummer of Airlie;
You will know the Reaper is coming for you.

1973

PROPHET OF DOOM

Believe me, I don't deserve this fate;
I walk through woods of hollow trees,
The earth is damp beneath my feet,
I'm cold inside and hungry.
The birds no longer sing.
Silence lingers in the air.
The babbling brook is dry.
The sky is black with cloud.
The path is paved with rotting leaves, for
All is dying.

The corn is brown, unharvested.
Flora by the wayside withers and droops.
The sun has gone, there is no light,
Covered are the woods by night.
Cold misty air, so sharp,
Rises from the ground.
No sign of life I see.
Deserted, the woodland waste
Decays outside the city gates, for
All is dying.

Leave me. It is already far too late.
The city streets are empty
And all is quiet.
The doors are locked and bolted.
No welcome greets a stranger passing through.
The echo of a woman's cry
Fades away as eyelids close.
No children playing,
No preachers praying, for
All are dying.

I slump beneath a blackened tree,
It's branches brittle bare.
The landscape is so desolate
It stabs my throbbing head.
Pains like arrows strike me quick,
I reel and dizzy
Have a fit.
While numbness floods my brain,
I too am feeling very sick as
All are dying.

My crooked smile splits bloated lips
As rain runs down the stricken tree.
Large acid drops and water drips
Are gently soaking all of me.
No shelter anywhere.
Am I the only one alive?
Has God deserted all of us?
This is no Eden, more Armageddon.
The land is flat and even
I am dying.

I kiss the ground on which I crawl.
The grass turns slowly black.
The skeletal trees are cracked.
Above, the thunder roars in triumph.
As lightning flashes down the barks
The hollow trees ignite,
Like torches in the night,
Giving out a warning glow
To anyone who doesn't know, that
All is dying.

Leave us you devils of mankind
Who torment us with your lust for power.
It is you who lead us to the brink
Of what might be Earth's final hour.
Time and time again you fight
For what you see as so-called might.
You fill our futures full of dread,
So do not mourn for me if you are left
And I am right, when all is dead.
This world is slowly going insane;
Our final hope must surely be
That one day Christ will come again.

1965

CREATION (HAIKU)

Change in a vacuum;
Something from nothing in space.
So what's the matter?

2011

IN HELL

I am broken,
    I am a shell.
I am empty,
    I am a well.
I am dying,
    I am a cell.
I am unlovable,
    I am in hell.

1974

11

ORANGE TANG

Orange juice
Morning marmalade
Buttered toast
Breakfast round the table.

Sun blessed trees
Spanish greengrocer
Jaffa world
Growing sweetly pliable.

Orange squash
Late noon pick-me-up
Quenching thirst
Pip-throats warmly viable.

Sunset fruit
So health refreshing
Bathed in taste
Gripped in tacky palms.

Peel the skin
Suck the vitamin
Tangy teeth
Release the balm.

1976

IN DEFENCE OF LOVE AND WAR

Rustling
Quills, and mating calls,
From a muster of peacocks,
Ostentatiously selling their selves,
Exhibiting aggression
In a colourful ritual,
Attracting attention.

Marching:
A form of walking,
Displaying military might
By rhythmic exaggerated actions,
Adding dramatic impact
Promoting pride and power,
Breeding security.

2018

13

MR. JONES

Mr.Jones smokes all he can.
His skin sports a nicotine tan
Which people think he gets on the Riviera.

Mr.Jones speaks with a stammer
Since his daughter, with a hammer,
Hit him between his legs around Cape Horn.

Mr.Jones plans well ahead.
He bought his wife a double bed
Because he did not like her sleeping on the floor.

Mr.Jones sits in his corner
Playing with his doll called Norma
Which, with heated breath, he inflates from time to time

Mr.Jones delights in malice.
He bought an old pretentious palace
With the rent money extorted from the poor.

Mr.Jones sits on his throne;
A second hand loo, all his own,
Made of gold he charges visitors to view.

Mr.Jones worships all he owns.
He lives in a million different homes
Wherever love of money is to be found.

Mr.Jones has even changed his name
Because it sounded rather plain.
Now he answers to the name Smyth-Jones.

1973

NO NEED FOR SALVATION

I don't want to be saved;
Not as I am,
Not as a man.

Eternal life must be boring;
All that time
Which would be mine.

I don't want to sing with angels;
I'm tone deaf.
I'd prefer to rest.

I wouldn't mind being God;
That would be fun,
For everyone.

We could do what we liked;
Do our own thing,
Create anything.

I would need unlimited powers
To build a heaven
I could be happy in.

Even then, I'd take it for granted
And get bored
With it all.

1975

THE LOST TRIBES

We know the whereabouts of Benjamin and Judah
But where are the missing ten lost tribes?
And what of the promises made by God to Israel,
Are they null and void? Did they not survive?

Did the tribes migrate across the whole of Europe
Then settle in these far off Western Isles?
Did their descendants take the Word of God to others
Spreading faith and hope to enlighten lives?

Did the Anglo Saxon Celtic speaking nations
Fit the role of a chosen people?
And when called upon to suffer sacrifice and loss,
Did they boast about it from church steeples?

Was Joseph of Arimathea the first to plant the seed
In this outpost of the Roman Empire,
By bringing Jesus at the age of twelve to live here,
As holy writ and legend so conspire?

Is God working out his purpose each successive year?
As a nation do we have a choice?
If so, our history and our future path are clear -
As spoken by the prophets with one voice.

2016

SENSES

Touch tells me you are here.
I can feel the shape of your body,
The warmth and smoothness of your flesh.
It tells me the air you breathe has motion.

Taste tells me what is bitter and sweet
When I drink and suck or eat.
I can taste your salty tears
And the fruits of your desire.

Sight gives colour to my life;
It brings proportion and perspective.
My eyes take pictures of your face
To store away in my memory album.

Smell distinguishes animal
From vegetable and mineral.
I can smell the fragrance of your hair
And the odour of your armpits.

Without hearing I would not know sound;
I would not hear the music in your voice
Or your knock upon my door,
Nor the rustle of your dress as you pass by.

There is a sixth sense which no one can define.
It makes us conscious of other things
The given senses can't detect.
Maybe the most important one of all?

We also have a sense of humour and of honour,
A sense of what is right and wrong;
A sense of achievement and responsibility,
A sense of our own importance and ability.

If all our senses worked towards a common goal,
Would the end result in common sense?
And yet with all our senses open to deception
How can we be sure of anything at all?

Our senses tell us what there may be
And where, and when, and how;
They do not provide any key at all
To why we are here, locked outside the door.

1974

TREAD SOFTLY

Where gods are,
Men fear to tread
In case they too are trodden on.
Even gods without legs
Are to be feared,
For they can tread on you
Without your knowing;
Until the weight of their burden
Is felt too late,
As you wander through the mire
Going your own way,
Searching for the gates
To Paradise.

1976

CUTTING A NEW IMAGE

In the theatre of dreams
With surgical precision
The surgeon, like a sculptor,
Fashions a new me.
In middle age
Nothing so becomes a man
As circumcision.
Fear not the rejuvenated image.

This primitive rite of passage
Which contrives to mark
Some barbaric, superstitious
Necessity in Man to become a man,
Is not for me.
Mine is not a symbolic act;
Needs must, that damaged cells
Be cut away to make all well.

Thus, I delight in my newly carved image;
Like taking off one's hat
To welcome a new dawn.
Alas, the cut is scant consolation
To female ritual victims,
Who realise far too late
That FGM results in their losing
Much more than just a little weight.

1997

HEAVEN

Is there a place somewhere above
Where dwells the Maker in His might,
Now growing old and white with beard,
Sitting, watching us below;
Patiently waiting, ever ready, quick to strike,
Guiding His flock by day and night?
Is this what we call 'Heaven'?

Is there a state of mind or being
So well defined, so near to bliss,
In which our senses reach nirvana;
So sharp, so sensitive to beauty,
Consciously growing more aware that this,
Like some supernatural kiss,
Is what we call our 'Heaven'?

It cannot be.
The first mocks God by making Him a man;
The second by making Man some kind of god.
Perhaps the answer lies somewhere between the two,
Or where they both do meet and merge as one?
Either way, I cannot find my 'Heaven'
And if I could, I think you'd find it hell.

1973

I HAD A DREAM

I had a vivid dream last night:
I went for a walk to take in the sights.
Streets and shops were mainly empty,
No crowds of people in a rush,
No one queuing for train or bus
But of things to do, there were plenty.

As there was no one else about
I went for a swim in the local river.
Once I was in I couldn't get out
So I went with the flow, all a'quiver.

Feeling all washed up my spirits sank.
In time I was dumped on a muddy bank.
Not the best of places to be -
By now I was dying for a pee.
I hunkered down on bended knee
Then a dog strolled up and peed on me!

An owl flew past at a roundabout
And knocked me down with a feather.
When I stood up I rolled about
Like a ship in stormy weather.

At last I made it all the way home
And saw the folly of those who roam.
Around the silent streets at night,
I'd learnt enough to see the light.
It was a dreadful dream, I do confide,
Which seemed much worse when I revived.
I woke in my bed, feeling oh so guilty,
All dripping wet and really filthy.

2016

ABRAHAM

Abraham was a man of faith.
Abraham was a man of grace.
Heard the call of the Lord
"Better go and leave this place,
Without a word".

Abraham left the City of Ur,
Took his wife, his goods and hers.
All the family and their friends
Took their camels, flocks and herds,
Without a word.

Abraham obeyed the Lord,
Trusted in his guiding hand,
Wandered through the desert plains,
Made his home in the Promised Land
Without a word.

Abraham was a man of faith,
Made the father of the race.
Heard the call of the Lord
"Abraham, Abraham, You'd better go,
Without a word".

1965

COME THE SPRING

Come the spring when maidens sing,
Come the day when winter has gone.
Then we'll hear the bluebells ring
And the birds mating songs.
Come the time when young men sow,
Seeds of love since times long ago,
Then we'll see every newborn,
Come the spring.

Come the spring we'll dance and sing,
Work and play to nature in song;
She will wear golden rings
In her hair all day long.
Come the night and shady moon,
Casting spells with magical tunes,
Then we'll hear every newborn,
Come the spring.

Come the wind to have its fling,
Come the rain when days are not long,
Dawns of dew, clear skies bring,
Leaves of green growing strong.
Come the sun and rainbows bright,
Linking Earth with Heaven's delight,
Then we'll greet every newborn,
Come the spring.

1974

SITTING IN SILENCE

I speak with my eyes.
If you look you cannot fail to see
The words I form.
Yet from my lips there is no sound.
A thousand thoughts pass through my mind
As we sit in silence saying nothing.
I sense the closeness of your body
But you do not move.
A mutual deafness fills our ears.
Inhibitions multiply our fears
And in my dreams I feel your tears
Soaking up the emptiness.

Won't you come into my world?
I view it from a distant star
Noting all it's faults,
Yet there is nothing I can do.
I see a million people pass me by
As I sit in silence saying nothing.
I know the pain and tragedy
Of life's lost cause:
As step by step men trudge the highway
Thinking night is day;
They take my world and do not pay
For stamping out its beauty.

All around me people stare
As if I'm standing naked in the sun,
Revealing all I have for them to judge.
Yet I am free and they are not.
Prisoners of themselves they fight for love
As we sit in silence saying nothing.
I sense their open mouths
And vile tongues
Spitting out their poisonous words.
The venom of the suburbs,
Gossip, flies as free as the birds
Feeding on all it can find.

Deaf and mute I watch
As you react to all around,
All ready to conform.
Do you really care what others say?
Are you chained to convention like the rest?
As we sit in silence saying nothing
I share your shame and pity;
Your hopes destroyed
Because you are afraid inside.
Your soul is open wide
For all to see what you try to hide.
Fear not. I will not speak.

Look into my eyes.
I do not have to say a word,
You know my thoughts.
A dreamer in his sleep forgets the time.
Eternal bliss, a lifelong yearning even yet
As we sit in silence saying nothing.
I sense your deep devotion;
Your happy smile
Shines through the window of my heart.
Have faith, we'll never part.
So look into my eyes and make a start.
Look now and tell me what you see.

1969

NORMAL SERVICE

Out of the darkness came the light.
With one look my thoughts were aroused.
In one act my anger was doused.
With one smile my world was made bright.
In one word my wrongs were made right.
With one kiss my life was restored.
In one breath I came back to life.

2016

BIRD PARADISE

Birds of Paradise
Caged in netted zoos,
Wired and snared
They lose their shine
And fade away in twos.

Faced with extinction
Herded together
Mated and paired
For their own good -
Never mind the weather!

Sad lifeless creatures
Lost in a strange land
Preserved for us
To pay to see -
Pound coins in captive hands.

1976

DRIFTING AWAY

You are drifting away from me
Like a boat which has lost its mooring,
Slowly, almost unseen,
Undulating with the water,
Receding, soundlessly.

Your mind vacillating, uncertain,
Lost in a dilemma:
Who to have, what to do,
Who to hurt -
Them, me or you?

With your loving you have created hatred.
With your demanding
You have deprived
Even those you love
Of a lifeline to cling to.

1975

THEY SAY

Sex, sordid sex.
"Oh my word!"

Dirty mucky yucky sex,
Filthy films and photos;
Porno pictures in one's head,
Sleazy scenes with screams.
"IT'S OKAY" they say.

Sex, horrid sex.
"Oh my Lord!"

Furtive fantasy sex;
Capture the rapture
With toys of joy.
Moments to treasure,
Love in the name of Pleasure.
"ENJOY" they say.

Sex, selfish sex.
"Oh my God!"

Sinful lustful sex;
Dominate and subjugate a mate,
Rough and tumble for a fumble,
Creams and lotions ease the motions,
Fighting basic instincts on a bed,
Wills aching to be led.
"OBEY" they say

Alas, I do not think I can.
I am inhibited and prohibited
Because of who and what I am.
I find sex rude and crude.

"YOU'RE A PRUDE" they say.

2012

DOUBTING THOMAS

Father Tom spent all his life preaching the good news:
Have faith or death, we have to choose.
The Gospel speaks of Paradise,
Much better than a cruise.

Tom was a travel agent sent unto the pews,
Issuing tickets to the few,
Guaranteeing ultimate bliss
And free insurance too.

One day old Father Tom consulted his GP.
The doc confirmed he had big C.
Did Thomas die in faith or fear
In so few weeks as three?

2018

JENNY THE GEM

She was a scrubber from Manchester.
She scrubbed everything wherever she went,
From John O'Groats to Cornwall and Kent.
They called her Jenny The Gem.

She scrubbed all the windows and all the walls.
She scrubbed all the doorsteps and all the floors.
She scrubbed all day and most of the night.
She scrubbed everything that came into sight.

She scrubbed for a time at a football club.
She scrubbed all the silver and all the wood.
She scrubbed all the players and answered their calls.
She scrubbed all their kit including their balls.

She scrubbed for a while at the public baths.
She scrubbed all the swimmers and made them laugh.
She scrubbed the pool with plenty of water.
She scrubbed the attendant for the money he brought her.

She gave up her scrubbing to marry a gent.
She enjoyed all his money until it was spent.
After having a child she went scrubbing again,
A first class scrubber, now her daughter's the same.

1973

NEW HOPE

Hope has a new dawn every day;
The sound of singing far away,
A footprint in the desert sand,
Smiles from a stranger in a foreign land.

Hope has new horizon faces
Lighting up the darkest places.
Like a traveller through time,
Hope is a servant of mankind.

Hope is the offspring we require
Born to the helpless to inspire,
Child of the embers of desire,
Raised like a Phoenix from a fire.

Hope has all the saving graces,
Kicking over all the traces.
When we encounter testing storms
Hope is a coat to keep us warm.

A coin cast in a wishing well,
Messaged bottle on ocean's swell,
When we have faith enough to float
Hope will arrive to help us cope.

On stormy seas of black despair,
Come guiding hands from those who care.
The Promised Land of every prayer;
God's lifeboat fit to take us there.

2018

BODY AND MIND

Three score years and ten
Is not a lot when looking back.
Body tells another story:
Says its been "a long time on the rack!"

Mind is younger, full of show
While Body's on a 'go-slow';
Wants to replay pleasant times.
Body's not having any of that!

Body, once the dominant part
Demanded urgent needs be met
And like a doting mother-hen
Mind met those needs without a sweat.

Now Time has changed the roles around
And Body is a burden and unwilling slave.

This temple of the soul and spirit,
Worn by the tides on a sea of sin,
Crumbles away with each experience,
While holy chrysalis grows within.

All charity stored and tender reared
To feed eternal life, so feared,
Is kept in Mind, to be released
When lovers once again will surely meet.

The speed of life deceives poor Mind
Who in his prime thought Time was slow.
"Hurry up!" he shouts to slothful Body,
"Time is catching up with us you know!"

1985

EYE OPENER

We meet again,
On waste ground.
Hopes rising,
The blood rushes
In gushes
Through blue veins.
Thunder pounding
Round my head.
Dilated pupils,
Suns eclipsed
Peer out of
Burning eyes.
Behind us and out of focus
Lies the debris of past desire.
Silent messages transmitted,
Received, recorded and replayed
Quicker than the speed of light,
Form a million impressions.
My eyes blink, uncertain.
The flesh on your cosmetic face
Seems to be creeping, weeping,
And falling in blobs to the earth;
Image destroyed in a stroke,
I see you for what you are.
I turn and rush for the waiting bus
As a bent coin slips from my pocket
And rolls away into the gutter;
Useless, worthless, lost for good,
Never to turn up
Again.

1976

EARTH, WATER, FIRE AND AIR

Earth is soft and fertile;
A bed in which grow seeds
Of grain, flowers, weeds and trees.

Water is wet and flows;
The source of life and power,
It creates and destroys at will by the hour.

Fire is hot and burns;
It transfigures and transforms,
Ashes to ashes and dust to dust.

Air is invisible all around;
It is free for us to breathe,
Both still or moving at gale force speed.

The earth needs water
And the fire needs air.
Nature needs them all, so I should care
While I am still here, they are still there.

1974

I'M A VANDAL

I'm a vandal,
I'm a wrecker,
I'm a breaker-in-two.
I'm a yobbo,
I'm a smasher,
I'm a nuisance to you.
I'm a wilful destroyer of beautiful things.

When I'm bored and frustrated
With nothing to do
I'll wander the streets
And get kicks with my feet
By mugging a woman or two.

When I'm tired and resentful
Of people like you,
I'll go with my mates
And get rid of my hate
By smashing a window or two.

When I'm scared and confused
By something that's true,
I'll carve out my name
And prove that I'm sane
By wrecking a car or two.

When I'm high and elated
By drinking a few,
I'll paint the town red
On blank walls like my head
By smearing a letter or two.

When I'm angry and violent
I'll damage what's new.
I'll skin a few cats
Or light fires with a match
And torch a building or two.

Whatever you state,
I'm proud to relate
I'M A VANDAL, mate!

1976

A SONNET TO ADAM

Before shadowy dawn I made a vow
To pay the debts of time, and needs repair.
Alone, I heard my lies denote despair;
Today, the voice of conscience takes a bow.
The stage is set to make amends from now
And players all assembled more aware,
Prepare the scene to end a Grande Affaire.
Insight: a curtain, slowly drawn somehow;
I touch your arm, an old reminder sign,
To draw attention more to what's in hand.
I must confess a frailty found in Man;
As Eve in Eden once betrayed her line,
The Fall is played again in every land.
Enjoy the fruits of love as best you can.

1982

ELIZABETH REGINA

Elizabeth, descendant of the Royal House of David,
A thread three thousand years long;
Crowned on the Stone of Jacob in the Abbey,
Anointed at her coronation by Archbishop Fisher,
The same as was King Solomon by Zadok the high priest,
Whose throne God promised, would last for ever.

Elizabeth, head of the largest ever Commonwealth of nations
These western isles, Cassiterides, once home to Druids,
Sanctuary to the ancient migrants from Assyria;
Ten northern tribes of Israel, who lost their way
Till they were led by God's firm hand to pastures new;
Selected to answer their master's call till their lives shall end.

Elizabeth, lifelong servant to her chosen people;
A missionary nation spreading word of the one true God.
A seat of justice and of majesty, democracy and charity,
Offering shelter to the homeless, helpless refugees.
May all who dwell in our fair and noble land be blessed
By Almighty God and His servant Israel and our queen.

2017

LOVE – HATE RELATIONSHIPS

Love
    Respect
        Parents
            Pride
                Fall

Down
    Out
        Count
            Chickens
                Hatch

Eggs
    Fresh
        Break
            Pastures
                New

Desire
    Familiar
        Contempt
            Envy
                Green

Peas
    Split
        Sides
            Opposite
                Love

Hate

1972

A DAYTIME NIGHTMARE

Demons of the night be gone
I care not for your dance or song,
Of torments, endless and severe.

Dawn approaches, dreams depart.
I must awake and play my part,
Expecting nothing in return but fear.

The days are long and tedious,
Each one alikened to the previous.
No respite from the jeering crowds I hear.

Devils of the day return
To tempt me, but their 'tempts I spurn,
'Tho mocking laughter fills my ears.

The urge to self-destroy eats up my mind,
Devouring all other thoughts I find;
Slug-slow my brain, no longer clear.

Deny me not the right to live or die.
I care not for your reasons why
The scoffers scoff and lechers leer.

If I must suffer now for what I'm not,
What need of God? It's best forgot.
No need for mystics, prophets, seers.

In bed my dreams are on the run,
Racing hither and thither, no place to rest upon.
I'm wide awake and out of gear.

With head in hands I sit around,
The record plays but makes no sound.
My head now spins as visions reappear.

I cannot put the world to rights.
I cannot even sleep at nights.
I cannot even taste the bitterness of beer.

Outside, the tides of fortune rise and fall.
The waves of wonder, wide and tall
Smash and crash against the seaside pier.

And on a boat I float upon the sea.
The stranger on the shore I see - is me.
So far apart and yet so near.

I reach out and shout with all my voice.
It echoes, bellows, round the coast.
A ghostly silence chills the air, all noise has disappeared.

A solitary boat across the bay is sailing.
The weather's bright, but inside me it's raining.
The shallow land is flooded by my tears.

On an island of my own I stand and stare,
Surrounded by the traps I've set in my despair,
Impairing all my steps and those to whom I'm dear.

People watch me pace my cage
And like a lion roar, in silent rage.
No sympathy nor help, they keep well clear.

They cannot understand my state.
They tell me not to worry but it's too late;
My name upon the wall is just a smear.

I wish no harm to anyone upon this earth.
No hatred in my heart I hold, nor mirth.
All life to me is sacred and all things I revere.

No more poetic words I'll write,
I have no more the will to fight.
The demons of the night to me adhere
And I have reached my life's nadir.

1967

ASPIRING FOOTBALLER

Striker Mike Cook
Was too concerned about his look.
Whenever in a position to shoot
He'd stop and clean his boots.

2018

A TONIC SO FAR

The bank was raided.
The robbers later fled
To their hideaway
With wads of notes stuffed in cases.

Except for Lartey,
Who had a cold and sneezed
And was quickly caught.
His cut was split among the rest.

Ray, the gang leader
Heard rumours Lartey knew.
One of them had blabbed,
So he called the band together.

Lartey's best friend Jude,
When accused, denied it,
Assuring the boss
''Do doh me Ray, so far Lartey dont doh!''

1978

COLIN McGREGOR RAE

On the twenty-fifth of November,
Nineteen seventy four,
At the thirteenth hour,
When the sky was overcast and grey,
Colin McGregor Rae
Breathed in his last breath,
Expired and died.

His wife kept vigil at his bedside
Gripping his icy hand
As the veil came down,
Dividing life from death, night from day.
She had no time to say
"Goodbye", but tired sat,
In silence cried.

Robust and strong but a year before,
A hearty, healthy man,
Suddenly struck down
As if from behind, leaving him dazed,
He clawed his crab-like way,
A convict condemned,
Caught to be tried.

He faced his trial without complaint
And took his tests in hope.
His courage stood firm
For nine long months he survived each day
Between life and death's stay
In purgatory pain
He lied to hide.

He loved his family, home and work.
An ordinary man
Who gave to his friends.
His great pleasure was walking Lyme Bay,
Especially in May.
He spent his birthdays
By the seaside.

He died at the age of forty-five,
When dreams are still alive.
In Axminster his grave is set,
His faithfulness by faith was met.
Whenever I'm on the beach and sight a crab,
Or see ash drop from a fag,
I remember the cancer, the courage and the days
Of Colin McGregor Rae.

1974

IN NATURE'S GARDEN

Flowers blossom in the summer sun
Then fade away in the evening shade.
Shadows of their former selves they droop,
The beauty of their youth betrayed.

In time each bloom will don its splendour
Bestowing colour on our mundane lives.
Scents and hues bombard our senses
Bringing joy to hearts and tears to eyes.

Every flower has its purpose.
Ask the bees that come to call.
When petals fold and day is over,
Remember loved ones when they fall.

2016

SAILING

I went for a trip on a sailing ship
And I thought I caught a glimpse
Of the water waving
As we tacked to and fro
Through the rain and the snow
Towards our haven.

We bobbed and bore towards the shore,
Full speed ahead we led the way.
The waves jostled and climbed
Like crowds of supporters
Urging us on with their roars
To an imaginary finishing line.

1972

PRIDE

In earlier times when men had clubs
And lived in caves,
Gay tribes
Found it difficult to thrive.
The Spartan army
Full of pride
Fought to the last
To keep their 'other halves' alive.
Heterosexuals too
Should celebrate with pride
The genes and chromosomes
They provide
To help the human race survive.

2017

IN A BEER GARDEN

Summer days, heat haze,
Sipping cider through a silver straw.
Fizzy pop, non-stop,
Consumed with thirst as bubbles pop
And sweat drops
From members of a beer garden.

Prize prats, fancy hats,
Paraded by those poor enough to bore.
Cloth shades, hand made,
By odds and sods of every type,
Gather aimlessly
In the corners of a beer garden.

Shouted words, unheard,
Euphoric outbursts erupt with glee.
Cackles sharp, dogs bark,
Peeling flesh displayed on shrinking earth,
Cracking cares apart
With bottle-toasting in a beer garden.

Red wine, mellow and mine,
In the bloodstream for a time.
Strong spirit run along
Quick enough to let me flee.
Shorts enough to get me home;
Ale aplenty do your duty,
Free the jailers and the jailed
In the confines of a beer garden.

1976

KNITTING

Click-click; click-click,
Go the knitting needles
As the old grey-haired woman
Rocks in her rocking chair
To and fro.
On the wall
The clock goes
Tick-tock, tick-tock,
As she knits.
Her mind wanders
As her hands draw
Semi-circles with the wool;
Up and down,
Backwards and forwards.
She is lost in the past;
Memories making
Patterns in her head.
She dreams of the future
Hoping all her plans
Will materialise,
Like the cardigan
She is knitting.
Click-click; click-click.
And time ticks by
As the clock
On the wall
Goes tick-tock, tick-tock.

1975

ONE AND ONE

I'm so glad to be, I just had to be
Here in your arms.
You're so good to me and your love for me
Shows in your charm.
Way up in the sky the clouds go whistling by
As the tears in your eyes run dry.
You make me want to fly
You take me up so high.
You give me so much fun
You are my chosen one.

I don't like to be, I've no right to be
So satisfied.
You're a dream to me and I love to see
Stars in your eyes.
Way down on the ground the wind goes whistling round
While the hopes in our hearts abound.
You make me jump for joy.
I'll gladly be your toy.
You're brighter than the sun.
You call and I will come.

I was slow to see, yet still hope to see
My Wonderland.
Love was dead to me then you said to me:
"Come, hold my hand."
Way over the moon, we'll dance and whistle our tune
When we tie the knot in June.
I'll give you a ring.
Together we will sing.
The bells will all be rung,
Our love songs all be sung,
As one and one make one.

1975

GAME

She beat you to me.
You had a lovely body -
Two arms and two legs,
But she also had a head,
Which crowns the lot,
Not just in Beetle Drive
But in the mating game.
My gain is your loss.
Remember that
Next time
The dice you toss.

1976

BEYOND BELIEF

Where were you in your teens and twenties?
The Gospels do not say.
You appear upon the stage
In a very mysterious way.

When baptised by second cousin John
In the river Jordan,
You meet as total strangers,
All normal recognition gone.

You started preaching in your home town.
Why did no one know you?
You must have worshipped weekly
Like any other local Jew.

Did your family not believe you?
Did it make you think twice?
When they came to take you home,
Because you claimed to be the Christ?

While walking through the rose garden
Of a busy psyche clinic
A damsel lounging on a bench,
Asked, was I a patient in it?
"No. It's a friend I've come to see".
"Hello", she said, "I'm Jesus Christ,
But the staff here don't believe me".

2018

BOA VISTA

The island, a "Boa Vista", in name and more;
Atlantic rollers thundering in from the west,
Exploding on the soft white sands along the shore,
Expending energy till they come to rest.

A "Good Sight" for sailing vessels seeking shelter
Trying to outrun dangerous tropical storms.
Early years saw cattle raised while shepherds sweltered
Under a blazing sun too hot to grow corn.

Later, the English came, extracting salt from sea.
Others produced ceramics and cloth to trade.
Today it is tourism; beaches, palms and turtles free;
A source of wealth for modern day pirate raids.

This once peaceful virgin island paradise
Has become a noisy hedonistic Mecca.
While the constant breeze quells thirst like ice,
Screaming children overheat and adult 'thieves' turn
wreckers.

2013

FRED

I knew you from the Med, Fred,
Your Dad was in the war.
I saw him filled with lead Fred.
Your mother was a whore.

I knew you as a Ted, Fred,
When you were young and coarse.
But now you are a Red, Fred,
And fight a different cause.

I knew you were well-read, Fred,
Your phrases such a bore.
Has everything been said, Fred,
Or is there any more?

Remember when you led, Fred,
The 'right to strike' excuse?
They lost their jobs instead, Fred
Your selfish ends to boost.

Remember your old shed, Fred,
Where once you beat up Bruce?
You left him there for dead, Fred,
For telling you the truth.

Remember when you wed, Fred,
She played you fast and loose?
You tied her to the bed, Fred,
And round her neck a noose.

Remember brother Ned, Fred,
Lay starving at your door?
You gave him crumbs of bread, Fred
And made him beg for more.

I know you have a head, Fred,
But do you have a heart?
The country you have bled, Fred,
By bloodless martial art.

I know you are well fed, Fred,
You drink your bloody fill.
The parasites we dread, Fred,
Are you and yours who kill.
Take note, we have not fled, Fred.
Pray God, we never will!

1977

SOME SAY OTHERS DO

Some say that Mary was a virgin
As the prophets foretold.
Others say she was a young maiden
Of marriageable age.

Some say she was made pregnant by a
Miracle - the Holy Ghost.
Others say she conceived naturally,
With her hymen broken.

Some say she mated with a soldier
In the Roman army.
Others say that Joseph was the Dad;
But Joseph denied it.

Some say she was an unmarried Mum,
A wilful, wayward girl.
Others say she was chosen to be
The mother of God's Son.

Legitimate or not,
It's not who people are, nor what they say,
But what they do and why, which matters.

1980

ASPIRING CRICKETER

All-rounder M. J. Cook
Scored his runs by strokes of luck.
He bowled with a very unique style
Causing his balls to bounce for miles.

2018

LUNAR ECLIPSE

As the sun sinks in the West,
Makes me think of home,
Where all the folk are resting
Till the coming of the dawn.

And slowly as the sun sets
I'm drawn to reminisce,
Thinking of my loved one -
It's her the most I miss.

The colours gently darken
And shadows lengthen more,
I reach out in the darkness
To what we had before.

The rising moon gives lovers
On half the Earth alone,
Hopes to be united
In "heavens" of their own.

2016

THE LOVING FOOL

There are men enough in Galilee
Who will tell you what you want to know of me.
They sing a song of sad lament
For all the ones who've loved and lost;
The man upon the cross whose flesh was torn,
Whose silent agony gave life to those unborn.
And I can share the cup he had to sup
For I am betrayed, rejected, led astray.
Down the passages of time I tread
Seeking a place to rest my weary head.
And no one cares that I could die
My barren life so useless I could cry.
Where is the life I long to live?
Where is the love I long to give?
Sing my song and sing it loud,
Deafen the dumb whose silence does deceive
The aching breasts of those who leave
Their loved ones far behind.
Strike the knife at the heart of stone
Which bled my ego, confidence and zeal.
Cut the stupid puppet's strings
And slit his throat so he cannot sing
The lies of love he sang to me.
If you should ever walk the plank
While feeling all at sea, with salty tears,
Stem the sickness in your stomach as it churns
And take the step to free yourself to be with me.
My finger tips long to caress
The parts of you I do not know.

My soul so trapped calls out to you,
The chains of bondage peel raw the flesh,
To free the loving fool inside of me.
And you! Can you watch the fool so taunted?
Can you turn your backs while he is tortured?
Or will you act before his ordeal is done?
You fool to watch the foolish die!
The man upon the cross, the fool did cry
"Forgive them. They know not what they do."
Know or not, they did the man to death.
The fool upon the cross you see is me.

1975

SWAN SONG

Super Mute Swan with crooked neck
Sitting on her nest of down
Tied by the instinct to survive,
Swaddling her cygnets five.

And on the coiling wind
Echoes of a bass guitar
Belting sounds conveyed by currents of air
Across silent fields to animal ears elsewhere.

Noise like the beat of a soldier's drum
Hammering the brain, smothering thoughts,
Blotting out both fear and foe
Projected from the darkness of the disco.

When I succumb, the urge to sing
Electrifies notes in my throat.
Pray that my chords be not too long
Nor my song too strong for the Swan.

1977

ALL SAINTS, KIRKBY MALLORY

Come, let us congregate in communal joy,
To celebrate this great Festival of Flowers.
Let All Saints be filled with lavish songs of praise
And old church bells ring to herald God's hour.

Man born of woman full of noise and woe,
Be still! Hark the silent witness of the flowers!
They toil not to adorn themselves in splendour
Nor don crowns of pride to advertise their power.

Rejoice in their richness and abundance of blooms.
Like our own frail flesh, holding goodness within,
They flourish then wither, colours slowly fade,
The pleasure they give, unstained by man's sin.

Flowers carved in cedar wood embossed in gold
Adorned Solomon's Temple, symbolically sound;
Tokens of victories, remembrance and love;
Gifts we can honour on Byron trod ground.

Feast eyes and keen senses on hues by the score,
Variety in texture, fragrance and line;
Each one unique like the family of Man.
There is much to be gained if we give them our time.

1991

DEEP IN THE NIGHT

Deep in the night when there isn't a sound
I lay awake and I look all around
Thinking of you and the love I have found.

I open my eyes,
I hear all your sighs.
I see a smile on your face,
I feel your warm embrace.

Deep in the night when I'm feeling down
I wonder if our love is profound.
Wherever you go, I worship the ground.

Then, time seems to fly.
Then, morning is nigh.
I'm woken by the sun.
My dreams of you are gone.

Time to get up and go;
Dreams which you'll never know,
Rising from deep in the night.
I know that we'll be together tonight.

Walking along I look at the sky.
Full is my heart, hoping you're mine.
I think of you and the love in your eyes.

Then, doubts fill my mind.
Then, I cannot find
Words to express my fears,
When you are nowhere near,
Deep in the night when there isn't a sound.

1968

WORTH

Let nothing mean too much
Or else our judgements pale.
Emotions highly strung may snap
When safety systems fail.

Let not the loss of hopes and dreams
Cause anger or frustration.
Beware ambition when unchecked
By prudent moderation.

Our sense of values may distort
When traumas strike us down.
Such dramas help us all to grow;
Pain has its pleasure found.

Every thing and one has worth,
Relationships are brittle.
Howe'er mundane a moment be,
Let nothing mean too little.

1996

COLD COMFORT

Your body turns cold at my touch.
It's not as though I ask for much;
A little tenderness now and then
Which any cock seeks from his hen.

Why brush me off like a pesky fly?
A needy child would sulk and cry.
Where has all our passion gone?
Where once was much, there now is none.

Age does not wither every need
And what is man without his seed?
Locked in a husk of ageing years
Unable to flee from potent fears.

We close our eyes to future loss;
Like a creeping overnight frost,
We wake to find a winter's dawn
Has numbed the feelings love has borne.

Emotions may snap like rubber bands
Requiring occasional relief by hands.
Treasure the lover who understands,
Who'll bring some warmth to an icy land.

2012

MAN'S BEST FRIEND

"A dog is a man's best friend"
Or so they say.
He's a good companion, reliable and true
With whom to play
Or share the loneliness of night.
A confidant,
Who will keep our secret thoughts
And never breathe a word to others.
He's a domesticated creature,
To be patted,
Pampered and fussed over like a baby -
As if it really mattered.
These canine members of the family
Are sometimes fed more nourishing meat
Than members of the human race.
They have more licence
Even on a leash
Than men, when he walks the streets
Or strolls the beach.
They sniff at anything they find
And cock a leg
Happy to piss on walls,
Lamp posts, trees and even people's shoes,
While his owner stops,
Waits and looks the other way.
He defecates on roadways, sidewalks,
Grass verges and even neighbours gardens.

His urine kills delicate plants and shrubs
Lovingly planted by others,
For us all to share as we stand and stare.
His faeces oft are trodden on
And spread about
For flies to feed and breed on.
Or left around for kiddies
Too young to understand
To pick and lick from inquisitive hands.
Given half a chance,
Dogs will copulate in public
While owner's say
"It's only nature's way, he knows no better".
Man's best friend is led away
And spoken to in tender, doting human terms.
Across the world, somewhere
A dog barks, a child cries, a stomach churns,
A dog bites, a baby dies.

1975

WORMS

Devil's
Flesh, ripple-ringed,
Sent to work underground
Tunnels in tombs of dead silence
For good.

To search
Buried bodies
And eat away decay,
Swelling jelly-soft bellies for
Blackbirds.

1976

END OF STORY

I was always an open book
Simple to read,
Transparent.
It was always in your look
To find a host
Who'd give you the most.
As I am quick to believe
You thought me easy to deceive,
But my trust was broken
When the first lie was spoken;
I knew then I would only grieve.
Never once the first to hug
Or offer me a lover's kiss,
You spoke only of material bliss.
Yet always keen to respond in kind
To whatever others had in mind.
You gave yourself freely
To anyone touchy-feely.
Hidden secrets tucked away
Never to see the light of day,
And yet I did indeed perceive
What time itself has proved-
Very sad but true,
I never really knew you.

2013

A BIT OF FUN

As I lie here in the sun,
I can dream about the one
Who has come to make my life
A bit of fun.

As I sit here in the shade,
I can dream about my trade
Which has made me millions from
My bit of fun.

As I lie here on the beach,
I can dream about the peach
Of a woman who provides
A bit of fun.

As I sit here facing South,
I can dream about the mouth
Which has truly granted me
My bit of fun.

As I lie here on the bed,
I can dream about the legs
Which have lain next to mine in
A bit of fun.

As I sit here in the raw,
I can dream about the bore
Who has always tried to spoil
My bit of fun.

Happy dreams
Which make my living
Gay and abandoned.
I'm resigned to enjoying
My little bit of fun.
In the sun
Or in the shade,
I've got it made
And I'm content,
To lie and dream
And set the scene
To film
My bit of fun.

1975

SKY

Above the clouds, a dazzling sun
Accentuates every hue of blue.
Below, mountains of moisture ascend in thermal puffs
Like seas of candy floss, bubble and stew.

Nimbus, frothing crests rear higher,
Curling themselves into cannonballs
Which Thor projects with a mighty roar
While gilt-edged and silver linings grace their fall.

Sky, battlefield of the spinning Earth;
High over heads where feral winds sway,
Among temperatures too cold for birth,
The triumphs of men may be blown away.

2009

SACRED MUSHROOM

Sacred mushroom make me a meal.
Hector's nectar helps me grow.
Atlas Mountains reach for the sky.
Mighty mushroom, tell me why.

Mandrake magic let me feel,
Pawing flesh so silky soft.
Satan's servant bound to die,
Mighty mushroom, tell me why.

Fate-plant of the open fields,
Nature's servant of the womb,
Teaching men to live and die,
Mighty mushroom, tell me why.

Countdown to destruction, flash of fire,
Burn the flesh-plant of desire.
Sow the seeds to raise a lie.
Mighty mushroom, tell me why.

Dust to dust my destination;
Ego-tripping god of revelation,
Who is the A and O of I?
Mighty mushroom, tell me why.

1972

IT PAYS TO ADVERTISE

It HELPS ME to sell the product.
A simple formula
To motivate the buying public.
Appeal to their need for

Health,
Efficiency,
Leisure,
Pleasure, or
Security. If that doesn't work, try

Modernity or
Economy.

Create the need
Provide the product,
Sell the idea,
Advertise.
It may not help you
But it HELPS ME
To take the money out of your pocket
And put it in mine.

1972

SHADES OF DR. ZHIVAGO

These are the words you've waited for,
Forbidden now as once before
By all not party to our needs:
And these, a last message;
Not of hope, for hope there's none;
But of faith made sure between us,
In the much-bewitching, wanton name of love.
By the rules of Man, made by men for men,
Even the condemned are granted a last wish;
And so it is I write to say
"Farewell", fair maid.
Soon I must depart to settle far away.
'Tis not by choice; the dying have no choice of death.
The hand of 'Fortune' which our meeting once did bless
Has torn our destinies apart for good,
Our paths no more to cross.
Alone we must await our fate.
Think not I failed you by my fickleness.
Even the mighty elements of wind and snow
Have their times to come and go.
Alas, they are assured they will return.
Not so go I, an exile from my place of birth.
What pains! What agonies upon itself
Doth bring the hungry heart,
So bent upon its own destruction!
And this I hold in my defence of honour
Which other men would call a fool's excuse:
The wilful ways of men and women
Will still pursue the quest for bliss,
To touch upon the magic wand
And conjure up some mystical dream;
To chance the eye and know that it exists.
I keep my word; I will not see you,
Nor speak to you again.
Where e'er I go I'll know you're near
And though silent, I shall hear your voice.

In the night I'll still your fears;
Though distant, I'll comfort send and stay your tears.
As no more of life to share,
No lovers parting waits for us.
No long last look into each other's eyes.
No fond embrace.
No lingering kiss to seal our prayers of safe return.
No words of comfort to console the aching breast.
No final touch of lovers hands,
No more to link in life.
No wave to bid "goodbye".
Nothing.
Only this can I offer as a parting gift;
A part of me, forever part of history.
Suffice it must, for both of us,
My Lara love.
And so fair maid, I say "Farewell".
'Twas not for nothing that I wrote you thus.
I won't forget my soulmate of this earth.
We met, we loved, with no regrets,
Privileged to have found and shared
A life which now is gone.
The sun still shines.
The moon reflects it's light.
And we must do the same to give them worth,
Or else we too deny our right to live
When all our rays of hope are gone.
And so, until the End, fair maid,
My Lara, Lara love,
"Farewell".

1973

ON HYDE PARK CORNER

By all the work I do
I can but help a few.
I stand alone amidst the mass,
I wait alone while others pass.
"To be or not to be?" I cry,
"It's up to you who pass me by."
This world of violence, hate
And earthly pleasures,
The love of truth
And truth of love
It never treasures,
How long will it last?

1960

BLIND FAITH

When I walked for the blind and their charity
Down through the valleys and over the tors,
The sun shone brightly on all before,
And the blind in their night showed a light to me.

Contrasts in Nature displaying disparity
Reflected the walkers who followed the cause,
When I walked for the blind and their charity
Down through the valleys and over the tors.

With love in their hearts they helped me to see
How blind was my faith in God and His lore.
Down through the dales and over the moors
I saw that they could so easily be me,
When I walked for the blind and their charity.

1972

ASPIRING PHOTOGRAPHER

Cameraman Cookie
When a rookie
Shot a mermaid in a scoop,
Only to find he had been duped.

2018

BOSNIAN BEDLAM

During the war in Bosnia
I saw three children at a gate.
Their heads locked in between the bars,
To get a better view of fate.

The inmates of the grey asylum
Watched transfixed the valley below.
Shells and bombs blew all asunder,
Smoke from fires began to billow.

Local villages razed to the ground,
Seen by lunatics on the hill.
Women driven out of their minds
By war atrocities which kill.

Evil breeds in the hearts of men.
Women don't start our modern wars.
Bedlam patients, secure within,
Observe the madness at their door.

2018

THE ARTIST AND THE MIRROR

The artist deals in what is truth and what is not.
He shows us what he can of life
By hanging up a mirror on the wall.
The glass, sometimes distorted, does not change.
People look and read and listen;
Gleaning what they may from what
Is spoken, seen or sung or written.

The artist is a teacher and he teaches what is real,
Reflecting life in all it's many forms
By hanging up a mirror on the wall.
The wall revolves and images appear.
People look and read and listen
Hoping they can see themselves in what
Is spoken, seen or sung or written.

The artist observes the world in which he lives
Creating new impressions for the inner eye
By hanging up a mirror on the wall.
The framework varies in size and depth.
People look and read and listen
Drawing false conclusions from what
Is spoken, seen or sung or written.

The artist, inspired by generosity and love,
Offers help to those who want to live
By hanging up a mirror on the wall.
He projects himself unwillingly, though
People look and read and listen,
Believing they can share his life from what
Is spoken, seen or sung or written.

The artist is a man apart, destined to suffer
The indignities of a martyr
By hanging up a mirror on the wall.
He gives himself to his calling, while
People look and read and listen
Knowing not the meaning nor the mysteries in what
Is spoken, seen or sung or written.

The artist proclaims his message to the world
Communicating all he possibly can,
By hanging up a mirror on the wall.
He hates the artificial, unoriginal or false, but
People look and read and listen
Passing superficial judgements on what
Is spoken, seen or sung or written.

1969

MISTAKES

The Romans crucified a man
Because the Jewish authorities
Accused him of claiming to be their king.
He said he was the Son of God.
Was he genuine, deluded, or a fake?
I'd love to know,
Because either he or they made a mistake;
And mistakes can kill
Both the body and the will,
Even of the innocent.

1974

ODE TO A COOK

The chef stood on the flaming deck
Feeling hot and flustered.
The galley fire consumed the ship
Because he'd burnt the custard.

2015

SMOKE SCREEN

You carried on smoking behind our backs,
Our money used to buy each pack.
For many decades you've had your fun
Deceiving each and every one.
A cigarette your closest friend,
Offering comfort, then cancer in the end.
As for us, we count for nought,
Killing yourself without a thought.
You watched while loved ones died in vain
And yet you play this poker game.
What cause in life ignites your need
For a daily fix of the toxic weed?
Is the love of family not enough
To halt this selfish suicidal bluff?
If only you could face each day and find
Reward enough to toughen up your mind,
Your body then may start to heed
The warning signs which make you feed
Upon the harmful lure of nicotine;
Then the fog of self-deception might recede.

2013

EACH TIME

Each time I see the sun is shining,
Each time I see the moon is rising,
I watch to see if you are crying
And wait to find out what you're hiding.

Each time I hear your voice a'sighing,
Each time I hear the babies whining,
I wait to find out what you're doing
And wonder who it is you're fooling.

Seems I've been a fool believing.
Seems it's only me you've been deceiving.
Now I find out that you're going,
Loving someone else without my knowing.

Don't know what it was went wrong.
Thought I was the only one.
Seems I've been a fool for trying.
Seems it's only time that I've been buying,
Now I've found out you were lying,
Telling me I was the only one.

1960

FROM IONA TO NORTHUMBRIA

Columba, the leader of the Irish mission to Caledonia,
Died in the summer of AD 597 at Iona.
In that summer there arrived in Kent
The historic Roman mission
Which came to renew the Word in Britain.
Sent by order of Pope Gregory the Great
And led by the saint to be, Augustine.

From the Humber to the Forth a pagan Anglo-Saxon
King Ethelfrith, ruled the two United kingdoms
Of Bernicia in the North and Deira in the South.
In 616 he was slain in battle
Driving the Britons into Wales as if they were cattle.
His four children were alas, left fatherless,
On the coast at Bamburgh, in the Royal castle.

The thanes consulted how to save the lives
Of Eanfrith, Oswald, Oswy and Ebba, and to decide
The destinies of these three princes and princess.
The boys were all sent to Iona.
We know not about the Princess Ebba.
In the course of time she became an abbess,
And the boys, good Christian Kings of Northumbria.

Meanwhile, Ethelfrith had been succeeded by Edwin of Deira.
He married Ethelberg of Kent and reigned over Northumbria.
She was a Christian, and in 627 he too accepted the faith.
Alas, at the battle of Hatfield in 633
A terrible disaster struck Christianity;
Edwin was killed by Penda of Mercia and Cadwalla of Wales,
Who ruthlessly ravaged the land, forcing the queen to flee.

Paulinus, who in 601 had been sent from Rome
To assist Augustine, took Ethelberg to Kent, her home.
They went by sea, while for a year the heathen victors
Dispensed persecution and destruction.
Eanfrith eventually returned to claim his kingdom
But was treacherously murdered by Cadwalla.
So the work of Christ remained undone.

In 634, Oswald, who had left Northumbria a pagan child
Returned, a man of thirty, zealous Christian, full of fire.
He fought Cadwalla at Heavenfield, near Hexham and won.
Before the battle his hands perfected
A large wooden cross which he erected.
Then he called his army to kneel and pray
To the true and living God and Christ the resurrected.

Oswald justly claimed Northumbria as his right
And requested help to convert his people to Christ.
He sent word to Iona for a bishop to open the door
But the first to arrive proved unsuccessful.
The missionary opportunity still lay in a cradle.
The second, a consecrated bishop came, named Aiden.
He was simple, gentle, wise and proved more able.

1975

CAPE VERDE ISLANDS

Ten volcanic islands in a corral
Offer protection from attack,
As huge Atlantic rollers sap morale
Of sailors when they are beaten back.

A jewelled ring; such a dazzling sight
Sparkles in the tropical sun.
Snow white rippled sands reflect bright light
Amid shifting dunes the prudent shun.

Constant trade winds sway verdant palms
While azure skies and turquoise seas
Display their Afro-Caribbean charms
Urging all to cast off care and wander free.

2013

COLOUR

If what I saw was brown
And you saw it as blue,
If we both knew it as pink,
Would you take it to be true?

If we were all colour-blind
And colours were not real,
Would it prejudice our outlook
Or change the way we feel?

1974

BLUE GUITAR

The winding howling twang
Of my blue guitar
Vibrates on a moonbeam
To the silent pockets
In your head
As it whines and it whines
Through the distant windows
Of your mind.
The echoes on the never-ending stream,
Gently floating and meeting
The rhythm of your heart-beat
With my guitar,
As it whines and it whines
Like a cat on a hot tin roof
Reluctant to leave
It's hopes behind.

1976

DO YOU CARE?

Do you care when you love me?
Or do you want to
Use me and abuse me
And tear me to pieces
Then cast me aside,
Leaving me to pull myself together
Later on,
And carry on
As if it hadn't happened?

1970

THE ISLANDS OF MEN

There are islands of men
There are oceans of love
And peace in the sky
Up above.
There are soldiers of sand
There are bombs made of snow
Washed up on the shore
Down below.
The islands of men
With their soldiers of sand
Keep growing each day
Till the winds come and blow them all away.

There are islands of men
There are mountains of hate
And war for a meal
On a plate.
There are houses of flesh
There are birds made of steel
Caught up in the fire
Of ideals.
The islands of men
With their houses of flesh
Keep rising each day
Till the flames come and burn them all away.

There are islands of men
There are rivers of greed
And dust in the air
That we breathe.
There are temples of sin,
There are gods made of clay
Built up from a pile
Of decay.
The islands of men
With their temples of sin
Keep falling each day
Till the seas come and wash them all away.

There are islands of men
There are babies of hope
And faith in the sails
Of their boats.
There are cargoes of salt
There are seas made of earth
Spread over the land
Of our birth.
The islands of men
With their cargoes of salt
Keep sailing each day
To a port which is never far away.

1976

INERTIA

Many
A
False
Step
Has
Been
Made
By
Standing
Still

1977

GO ON, TRY IT

When I was out with my love
He said "Come lie with me".
I looked at the sky above
And he asked me if I would,
Saying, "Go on, try it, go on".

A friend whom I liked a lot
Said "Share a joint with me".
She told me the stuff was hot
Before handing me some pot,
Saying, "Go on, try it, go on".

A man in The Rising Sun,
Said "Have a drink with me".
I told him I was too young
But he bought me coke and rum
Saying, "Go on, try it, go on".

Some people I know so well
Think I should be like them.
They cheat and they lie like hell.
My soul they'd love to sell
Saying, "Go on, try it, go on".

Oh no, no, no, to each and every one.
I said I wouldn't do it,
I couldn't tell my Mum.
I want to go to heaven
So I try to do no wrong.

1965

84

NEWS IN PAPERS

News is now;
Tomorrow it is history.
News is facts;
Though misleading they may be.
News is people;
Who, without the how or why.
News is action:
Wars, murders and disasters.
News is fun:
Pin-ups, babies, sport and stars.

News is photographs and words.
News is 'REAL' (with a question mark).
No one argues with a camera
When it flashes light on dark.
Different headlines, different meanings;
Captions tell us what we're seeing.
Not for the reader to decide.

The news of our times
Arrives with the mail
Express fast.
Guardians of truth
Mirror the facts
About the people.
Biased observers
Telegraph tales
As we bask in the sun
And read about our favourite star.

1973

THE WALL OF TIME

The wise remarks of men made famous by their words
Stand in line upon the Wall Of Time for all to read.
The world looks on, not knowing what the letters say,
For time has passed them by and people rot away.
The words upon the Wall spell out:
"WE LOVE TO LIVE AND LIVE TO LOVE."
So come, forsake all else and you will gain the world
By giving all you have to give.
Immortal phrases scribed by men of old,
Inspired by unknown people, places, things,
Remain when their contemporaries are dead and gone.
We see a part, the whole moves on,
Until the days of Revelation dawn;
When all the mysteries of life shall be revealed
And then the people by the Wall will understand.
All love once lost, the world will mourn.
The Wall Of Time, eternal in its glory, spirals
Upwards to the heavens, winding higher
With ever-increasing circles, it surrounds
The universe of distant sights and sounds;
While senses, mortal, fallible, untrue,
Inform us that the knowledge which awaits
Inside the gates of space, beyond this day and hour,
Is purified with every heart and mind made new.
The path around the Wall is littered with the mounds of bones
The empty shells of genius once used to build the words
"WE LOVE TO LIVE AND LIVE TO LOVE."
Come, view them from above,
Then shout them out and hear the echo-call.
The Earth may shake, foundations rock,
And all may be destroyed, except
The Wall Of Time, for that will never fall.

1972

TESTING TIMES

Education is an ancient sacred cow.
Every pupil must be able to take a bow.
To suit the chancers
You can guess the answers;
With multiple choice, exams are even harder now.

2013

THE END OF PRIDE

Bands of light flash blind the eyes,
Across the mind a thought inscribes
A memory; a vision seen, interpreted
By knowledge gained from past experience.
Corrupted, our innocence turns black.
The swollen grains of crops become
So large that senses, cold and numb
Give out: the harvest been and counted;
The autumn leaves in loose-knit piles, ignited.
The fires of hell released to fly
In gusts of wind which light the sky
Bright red; the golden dusk diluted,
And colours run before bleary eyes, unblended.
The crooked road of life bends back
The bones of those who lack the strength;
The anguish on the face, disjointed,
Becomes a mask of doom undaunted.
Where freedom grows the dove descends,
The shackles of time transcend
All glory; the proud who worked to win promotion
Find in their death no self-approbation.

1973

ENRAPTURED ENTRAPMENT

Deep in the grasp of a crisp winter's night
With stars overhead glistening bright
We lay side by side in a luxurious bed,
The lamp in the room glowing softly red.
I'm wrapped in the warmth of your body next to mine.
In the peace of the moment we have lost all sense of time.
Our senses are awakening in full anticipation
Of what we are to share employing every stimulation.
My eyes search yours firing arrows of desire
Aimed in hope, to set your loins afire.
Romantic music fills the air and soothes the ear.
Sweet melodies of love release a tear.
You find my hand and gently fold it in yours,
Secure the soul as you open up the doors
To the pleasures of the flesh which wait in expectation,
Rising to be freed and shown true appreciation.
I move my head towards your tender lips
And my blood flows fast as I caress your slender hips.
A smile lightly plays upon your face.
Your eyes are closed as we embrace.
I whisper softly words of humble adoration,
While erotic thoughts run wild in my imagination.
I nibble your neck, your ears, your heaving breasts,
Then run my fingers down your back and up your legs.
All modesty abandoned you urge me on for more.
Your sensuous body cries out to be explored.
You sway and swoon and wriggle and writhe.
With arms outstretched you start to sigh.
Then gently I reach down to touch your clitoris.
Your world explodes and body senses flip.

We rest awhile, then slowly start again as new,
The flames of lust aroused as if on cue,
Our bodies now in time and filled with wild emotion
Play out the tunes of love with deep devotion.
In perfect rhythm we proceed to fuck
As every muscle, nerve and sinew runs amok.
You take me out, you lead me in;
Your open lips so moist, so warm, so soft within.
Erect and stiff I throb with life,
With you submissive, willing, juicy ripe.
The chords of harmony play out
Until in ecstasy we scream and shout:
"Faster" to the climax felt in spasms
Till final thrusts erupt in orgasms.
Drained of our life-force but full of elation
We collapse all spent in our exultation.
Then in silent rapture, our legs entwined,
We lay together, joined in body, heart and mind.
In Disney style around the bedside table lamp
A frantic moth flutters in a dizzy dance,
It disappears as if in a puff of smoke,
It's suicidal antics, the result of a cruel joke.

2015

LIVING LANGUAGE

Language is a life-long sentence for Man,
Made up of letters, words, paragraphs
And chapters of communication,
In the ever-open pages of the
Book of Life;
Punctuated only by illness
And death.

1977

PEOPLE ASK ME WHY

As I walk about the town
Feeling like a foolish clown,
People stop and ask me why
You have said goodbye.

I think of our first kiss,
You touched me to the core.
What kind of life is this,
Now we shall meet no more?

People who are they to see
How much you meant to me?
People, who are they to know
That I still love you so?

I think of our last walk.
You said that we were through.
Your love was idle talk.
Now you love someone new.

1960

PUSS PUSS

She lay on the thick woollen pile
Of the carpet in front of the fire,
With her legs outstretched
And eyes half closed,
Waiting to be petted.
I knelt down beside the feline creature
So that I could touch her.
And with my palm I stroked
And caressed her silky hair,
Thinking "Oh, what a lovely pussy.
What a lovely pussy you are!"
She purred with contentment
Licking my hands,
Expressing her joy.
Later, she rose to leave the room,
Her lips half-open in a wicked smile.
And when she reached the door
She turned her head
And cast a knowing eye
In my direction.
Then, did I hear her sigh
And softly say
"Goodbye"?

1975

STEPPING OUT

One step
Out of the black void
To a mass of gas cloud.
One step
To explode
To form a sun star.
One step
Spun off the sun
Like clay from a potter's wheel
To harden to a planet.
One step
When the Biomagician
Cast his spell
To produce an amoeba.
One step
To flip a fish
One step
Out of the sea,
Ditched on a beach
And a freak to survive.
One step
To a reptile,
Cold blooded and ugly.
One step
To a mammal,
Warm hearted and cuddly.
One step
To a Homo sapien.
One step
To fly in outer space.
One step
Into a black hole for eternity.

1976

THE CHARMER

What words would you like
To hear me say?
I say whatever pleases
Other peoples' ears.
It pleases me to please them.
They like to be teased.
To be pleased
By me and my words.
They think I'm such a pleasant fellow
But my words are just words;
Hollow words,
Which sound nice to the ear,
To those who are near.
I am a fraud, a dummy,
A mouthpiece only
Few can afford,
Programmed to please.
I perform with effortless ease,
Without thought,
Without meaning
Without shame.
It's all a frivolous game
And my aim doesn't matter.
I more than influence to deceive,
More than flatter,
More than persuade.
No need for me to batter
My willing victims into submission.
At the end of the day
I always get my own way.
"Oh, charming!"
I hear you say.

1996

AT FIRST SIGHT

That first glance,
That first spark,
That surge of pure elation;
Desirous to possess such beauty,
Such perfection in another.
Like a miracle of Nature,
Difficult to comprehend,
Or reason How? Or Why?
The welcome in your eyes,
Your luscious lips
Which softly mouth "Come in",
Invite a confident response,
Positively charged.
Then to find our bodies faultless fit
To form a channel
For our unadulterated lust
Through which great tidal waves
Of passion roar
Like the Severn river's bore.
To fall in love, so commonplace,
Requires a special time,
A unique face,
For that first glance
And that first spark
Which quickens the heart.

Gradually, over time we learn
That falling out of love, in turn,
Is just as easy.
For relationships to last
We need to study what has passed.
Love is neither falling in nor out,
But 'doing' is what it's all about.
Commitment is an act of will.
Caring, a duty to fulfil.
Immature, our "love" is wild,
And lust alone is not enough
To raise a child.

1996

FLIGHTS OF FANCY

When I was a child in infant school
Seated at my hard wooden desk
I was mesmerised by a spinning globe
Of places picturesque.

I never thought that I would see
Those far off lands and seas for real,
But now that world beyond the classroom door
Air travel has revealed.

2013

SLEEPY BAG BLUES

When you take the girl of your dreams
And camp out for the night,
You might wake with a fright
When you find she's not what she seems.

She rolled up draped in retro rags.
God knows where she had been,
With her spray-on tanned sheen
Posh make-up and designer bags.

Retiring to rest at sundown,
I just didn't want to know;
Her breasts were sagging low
And uplift bra and corset strewn around.

When at last she was fast asleep
She started snoring loud.
I touched her but couldn't rouse
Even the bottoms of her feet.

When she woke up in the morning,
I clocked her standing there
With curlers in her hair,
All bleary-eyed and yawning.

Her spare tyres wobbled up and down.
A fag dangled from her mouth
As she shuffled about,
Moaning we were on bumpy ground.

Be on your way, soon as she says
Camping just isn't her scene.
If she stamps and she screams,
Then tell her you're actually gay.

The camp was a test
And the tent was a mess.
The sleepy bag blues
Come on when you lose
The girl of your dreams
Who's not what she seems
And you wish instead
You'd stayed home in your bed.

1972

TAKE IT OR LEAVE IT

When I am dead
I hope it will be said
"He could write a poem or two";
But when you've tasted three or four
And cannot stomach any more
Perhaps it would be best
To leave the rest
Unread.

2011

NOT CRICKET

It wasn't cricket,
Thought the bowler
As he ran up to the crease
And bowled the last ball of the over.

He had finished with her -
Though he had made promises
And she was expecting his child.

"Over" shouted the umpire.
True,
Thought the bowler
As he continued playing the game.

The crowd of spectators applauded their idol -
He'd bowled another maiden over.

1971

BOOK ENDS

I'm beginning to feel somewhat dejected;
Book sales showing worse than poor.
A lifetimes work and effort rejected,
Nobody knocking at my door.
This is the downside of being creative;
Needing support till you feel restored.

2015

NOBODIES

Fame does not preserve us
Nor faith secure us.
We strive to keep ourselves alive
By work and play we make our names,
Yet at the end we're all the same
By all becoming
"No-bodies".

2017

MY WILL

If you should ever find me
Please don't leave me be.
Pick me up and read me
Until you've had your fill,
Then pass me on to others;
For that is what I will.

2018

AND SO TO BED

No energy left with which to fight
Even after a restful night.
I'm left to ponder the way ahead,
What further tests before I'm dead?
Remaining positive, an uphill slog.
Easier to say than cut through fog.
Uncertainty a certainty day by day.
Humour, a pick-me-up in every way.
Step by step I tread the lengthening miles.
Do loved ones see the pain behind my smiles?
Stroke by stroke I swim against the tide
As I strive to keep their hopes alive.
I'm quite prepared to meet my fate
And whate'er awaits at heaven's gate.
My time grows shorter with each day;
Unlike a child who'll stay and play.
When bedtime calls to count the sheep,
I'll gladly go without a bleat.

2016

ACKNOWLEDGEMENT

I will be forever indebted to the following people for their help and encouragement in my early years of writing; the late George N.G. Smith, MA, Vice Principal of the College of the Venerable Bede, Durham University in the 1960s; the late Howard Sergeant MBE, promoter and publisher in the 1970s; the late Charles Causley, poet and teacher in the 1980s.

In more recent times I am extremely grateful to all those who have provided encouragement and support, especially those who posted positive and appreciative reviews on the internet. Namely, Patrick Martin, Joan Wedgwood, Thelma Clarke, John Hind, Dorothy Bambridge, Judith Bell, Tricia Jardine and Bill and Joan Watson. Words are not enough to express my gratitude.

This final anthology, 'Serendipity' will not be on general sale. It is a limited private edition of 100 copies, intended only for family and friends, plus a few charity shops to whom I donate a few copies of my work.

Collectors will be interested to learn that I was reliably informed that a copy of my first anthology, 'Stepping Stones', published in 1975 with a RRP of £0.60 pence, was sold in May 2018 for £227.14, by Ergode Books in Texas, USA.

Finally, I wish to thank Gail Tomkins and her team at Virtual Admin UK for self-publishing 'Serendipity' on my behalf. They have been most diligent and helpful in producing such a fitting "final curtain" to my poetic endeavours. Thank you to one and all.

M. J. Cook

APPENDIX

Books in which the above poems were first published:

STEPPING STONES (1975)

1   *Colour*
2   *Drifting Away*
3   *Earth, Water, Fire And Air*
4   *Knitting*
5   *Mistakes*
6   *No Need For Salvation*
7   *Sacred Mushroom*
8   *The Artist And The Mirror*
9   *The End Of Pride*

REFLECTING IN THE SUN (1976)

1   *A Bit Of Fun*
2   *A Daytime Nightmare*
3   *Blue Guitar*
4   *I'm A Vandal*
5   *Orange Tang*
6   *Senses*
7   *Sitting In Silence*
8   *Stepping Out*
9   *Tread Softly*

OF FAITH AND FORTUNE (1977)

1   *Abraham*
2   *Bird Paradise*
3   *Blow It*
4   *Colin McGregor Rae*
5   *From Iona To Northumbria*
6   *In A Beer Garden*
7   *Living Language*

COLLECTED POEMS (2015)

SELECTED POEMS

UNPUBLISHED

PUBLISHED ELSEWHERE

Some other publications in which my poems have appeared:

1   *20TH Century Poets, published by Regency Press, London and New York, 1974.*
2   *The Health Education Journal, 1975.*
3   *Axminster News, 1976.*
4   *Current Events, India's Journal on World Affairs, Dehra Dun, India, November 1976.*
5   *The Countryman, Oxford, 1976.*
6   *The Inquirer, London, in 1976 and 1978.*
7   *Writing, Winter 1977 and Spring 1978 editions, Fowey, Cornwall.*
8   *Caritas, Vol 46, No. 42, Co. Dublin, Eire, Autumn 1980.*
9   *Chard 750: A Commemorative Anthology of Selected Poems, published by Dillington Writers Circle Chard, 1985.*
10   *Winter Ensemble, published by Arrival Press, Peterborough, 1992.*
11   *Voices On The Wind, published by The International Society of Poets, Whitstable, Kent, 1996.*
12   *Eternal Faith, published by Triumph House, Peterborough, 1997.*
13   *Fourth World Review, in October 1997.*
14   *The Teacher, November 1997.*
15   *Moments of Inspiration, published by United Press Ltd, 2016.*
16   *NHS Patients In The Waiting Room Charity, 2017.*
17   *International Poetry Digest, August 2018.*
18   *The Nightingale Poetry Journal, March 2019.*
19   *Dandelion Arts Magazine issue 65 Spring/Summer 2019.*